Wisdom of the Golden Goose

Wisdom of the Golden Goose

A Jataka Tale

Illustrated by Sherri Nestorowich

DHARMA PUBLISHING

First published 2002

Second edition 2009, augmented with guidance
for parents and teachers

Printed on acid-free paper

Printed in the United States of America by Dharma Press
35788 Hauser Bridge Road, Cazadero, California 95421

9   8   7   6   5   4   3   2

Library of Congress Cataloging-in-Publication Data

Wisdom of the Golden Goose : A Jataka tale

(Jataka Tales Series)

Summary: A goose is trapped but willingly goes to the palace, bringing joy to
the queen and reminding the king to be grateful for his good fortune.

Jataka stories, English. [1. Jataka stories]
I. Nestoriwich, Sherri, ill. II. Series
BQ1462.E5 W56   2002   294.3'82325—dc21   2002031486

ISBN 978-0-89800-434-2

Dedicated to children everywhere

Once upon a time a king named Bahuputraka lived with Khema, his queen, in their palace in the city of Benares, in the far-off land of India.

In their realm, upon a distant mountainside, lived a magnificent royal goose. As the goose watched over his flock of ninety thousand geese, his feathers shone in the sun, just like gold.

One night, the queen dreamed that the golden goose came to the royal palace. He sat himself on a throne and spoke to her with a voice that sounded like the tinkling of a golden bell. Queen Khema listened to his words with delight, but a few moments later the goose spread his wings and flew away. In her sleep the queen cried out, "Do not go! Please, do not leave me!"

She called out so strongly that she woke herself up. The dream had been so vivid and her wish to hear the golden goose's words was so real that she felt faint with longing. The following day she was unable to leave her bed.

Seeing her weak and pale, the king asked the queen, "Please dearest, what would make you well again?" She told him of her dream and said, "I am sick with the desire to see the golden goose. Listening to his words of wisdom is the only thing that can make me better."

The king convened his ministers and said, "The queen wishes to see a golden goose. Is such an unusual creature to be found in my kingdom?"

"Yes, sire," they replied. "A golden goose leads the flock of geese who live on the mountain called Peak of the Mind."

"Just so!" said the king. "We will make a lake near that mountain and plant delicious grain at its shores. When the geese come to eat the grain, one of my hunters can easily capture the golden goose. Until then let no man, woman, or child go near the lake and frighten the geese away."

The lake was made as the king had ordered. When the grain around it was ripe, the golden goose led his flock to the shores and the geese began to feast.

Instead of joining in the meal the golden goose watched over them from a small hill nearby. In his concern for the flock's safety, he did not notice the rope snares that a hunter had hidden in the grass. Suddenly he stumbled into a snare and felt it tighten around his leg. He was trapped.

He remained still, waiting until all the geese had eaten their fill. Then he gave a sharp cry and the flock took flight instantly. Only one goose looked back: the faithful Sumukha, whose face shone with the beauty of loving-kindness. Seeing his friend caught in a snare, Sumukha set aside all concern for his own safety and flew to his side.

As the hunter ran up to secure his catch, Sumukha flew toward him and cried, "Our leader is virtuous and wise. He is our protector. He always cares for the safety of the flock and now he himself is in danger. O, hunter, please do not harm this greatest of birds!"

Greatly surprised, the hunter said to Sumukha, "There go the other geese, full of fear. Yet you, brave and wondrous bird, chose to stay here and risk your own life for the sake of the golden one. Tell me, why should I spare him and set him free?"

Sumukha answered, "He is my companion, my friend, and my king. He is as dear to me as my own heart. There is no way I could ever forsake him, even if you threatened to take my life!"

"If I were to bring harm to such an amazing bird," the hunter thought, "terrible harm might come to me too. What do I care for the king's reward? To be sure they will live, I will set them both free."

The hunter reached down, untied the rope and said, "Golden one, you are free. Fly away!"

The golden goose made no attempt to escape. Calmly facing the hunter he asked, "Did you catch me for yourself, or did you act at someone's request?"

"I came on the king's orders," said the hunter. "The queen wishes to see a golden goose like you. She became ill and may even die if her wish is not fulfilled."

"Then tie me up again," said the golden goose, "and take me to your king and queen."

The hunter cried out, "My friend, one never knows what a king will do! Beware! Really, I fear for your safety."

"Why?" asked the goose. "If I can make friends with you, can I not also make friends with your ruler? Do not worry about my safety and take me to your king."

When the golden goose and Sumukha arrived at the palace, the king and queen were overcome with joy. The king placed the golden goose on a golden perch and gave the geese honey and fried grain to eat and sweet water to drink. Then he invited the golden goose to speak his words of wisdom. In reply, the golden goose enquired politely,
"Does the king have riches and good health? Does he rule wisely and well? Are his people happy and their fields full of grain?"

"Yes," answered the king. "I possess both riches and good health, and I do my best to rule wisely and well. My good people are prosperous and our fields are full of excellent grain."

Then the goose went on, "Is your majesty's court free of troubles? Are your enemies far away?"

The king replied, "There are no troubles within my kingdom and court, and no foes can harm us here. Our enemies are like the shadow in the south, which never grows."

Again the golden goose asked politely, "And your queen, is she sweet of speech, patient, kind, and generous?"

Pleased, the king responded, "Yes, my queen is sweet of speech, patient, kind and generous to everyone."

"O great ruler!" the golden goose went on. "Are your children honest and kind, always responsible, quick to cooperate and willing to help?"

"Yes," said the king, "I am blessed with many good children. They are sincere and kind, and eager to help. Please tell me how to counsel and guide them, as they surely will take your advice."

Upon hearing this the golden goose said, "Tell them to choose their words with care and always do what is right. Whether we are kings or servants, we must learn to speak with kindness and be good to everyone. Rich or poor, we can develop such good qualities that others will trust us and follow our example. As our wisdom grows, our actions can light the way like bonfires in the night. O king, cherish your children and shower them with love each day, and they will grow upright and strong, like young plants watered by a healing spring rain."

All night long the king and queen listened to the wise words of the golden goose. Their minds became peaceful and their hearts filled with joy. At dawn, the golden goose and Sumukha, his friend, wished them well and returned to their flock on the mountainside.

My page

Colored by _____

The Jataka Tales nurture in readers young and old an appreciation for values shared by all the world's great spiritual traditions. Read aloud, performed and studied for centuries, they communicate universal values such as kindness, forgiveness, compassion, humility, courage, honesty and patience. You can bring this story alive through the suggestions on these pages. Actively engaging with the stories creates a bridge to the children in your life and opens a dialogue about what brings joy, stability and caring.

Wisdom of the Golden Goose

One night queen Khema dreams about a golden goose. Her wish to see the wise goose in reality is so strong that she becomes ill. The king orders his hunters to trap the golden goose, the leader of a large flock of geese high in the mountains. The goose's best friend stays with him and begs the hunter to spare the golden goose. However, the golden goose does not want the hunter to be punished for disobeying his king. Refusing his freedom, he asks the hunter to take him to the royal court, where he advises the king and queen to appreciate their good fortune and to teach their children the importance of loving kindness to all.

Key Values
Compassion
Loving kindness
Goodness

Bringing the story to life

Engage the children by asking at the turning of a page: "What do you think will happen next?"

Asking questions about the events and values in the story will deepen their understanding and enrich their vocabulary. For example:

- Why does queen Khema become ill?
- Why would the golden goose refuse his freedom?
- What is the golden goose's advice to the king?
- Do you have a friend who you can always count on?
- How would you feel, being challenged like the golden goose, to go into the king's palace?

Discussion topics and questions can be modified depending on the age of your child.

Learning through play

Children enjoy trying out new ideas, using all five senses to make discoveries. After providing the materials, the time and space for play, encourage their creativity and watch them explore. Play with the characters:

- Have the children color in or draw a scene or character that intrigues them. Then invite them to talk about what it means to them, and explore the key values of the story.
- Make masks for each character in the story.
- Paint the masks together and decorate them.
- Let each child choose a character to impersonate. Imitate the voices and bring the qualities of the golden goose, Sumukha, the hunter, the king and queen to life. Then switch roles.
- Display the key values somewhere and refer to them in the course of the day,
- Make up a story about someone in trouble and how a friend comes to the rescue.

Active reading

- Some Jatakas include difficult concepts. You can prepare by going over the story first yourself. By reading it to the children two or three times and helping them to recognize words, you encourage them build vocabulary.
- Hearing the same story with different and sometimes exaggerated voices for each character will captivate the child.
- Integrate the wisdom of the story into everyday life. When tempers flare or patience is called for, ask not just the child but also yourself what the golden goose might say in this situation.
- Carry a book whenever you leave the house in case you have some extra time to read.
- Talk about the story with your child while you are engaged in daily activities like washing the dishes, getting dressed or driving to school.
- Display the key values of the story somewhere visible and refer to them regularly in your daily interactions with the children.

Names and places

India: The source of many spiritual traditions and the background of most of the Jatakas (accounts of the Buddha's previous lives). People seeking wisdom have always viewed India's forests and jungles as favorable places for solitary retreats. The Buddha taught the Jatakas to clarify the workings of karma, the relationship between actions and results.

Benares: A holy city in North central India, on the river Ganges. One of the most ancient cities in the world, it is also known as Varanasi.

Bahuputraka: The king's name means "father of many sons."

The Jataka Tales are folk tales that were transmitted orally, memorized and passed from generation to generation for hundreds of years. We are grateful for the opportunity to offer them to you. May they inspire fresh insight into the dynamics of human relationships and may understanding grow with each reading.

The Jataka Tales are for children aged three to eight

JATAKA TALES SERIES